MIRRORUM · SIGNALIS · MANOUVRIT

MINISTRY OF
TOP GEAR

TopGear

THE ALTERNATIVE HIGHWAY CODE

MIRRORUM · SIGNALIS · MANOUVRIT

MINISTRY OF
TOP GEAR

TopGear

THE ALTERNATIVE
HIGHWAY CODE

Compiled by
Richard Porter and Paul Powell
on behalf of the
Ministry of Top Gear

BOOKS

10 9 8

Published in 2010 by BBC Books, an imprint of Ebury Publishing,
a Random House Group Company

The Random House Group Limited Reg. No. 954009

Addresses for companies within the Random House Group can be
found at www.randomhouse.co.uk

A CIP catalogue record for this book is available from the British
Library.

ISBN 978 1 84 990027 0

Commissioning editor: Lorna Russell
Project editor: Caroline McArthur
Art Direction and Design: Charlie Turner
Copy-editor: Ian Gittins
Illustrations: The Comic Stripper
Production: Antony Heller

Colour origination by: Christopher Rowles
Printed and bound in Germany by Firmengruppe APPL, Wemding,
Germany

To buy books by your favourite authors and register for offers, visit
www.rbooks.co.uk

CONTENTS

INTRODUCTION

Welcome to the *Top Gear Alternative Highway Code*. If you are learning to drive, this book will provide all you need to prevent you from doing anything useful before your driving test tomorrow morning. If you are already a qualified driver, the *Top Gear Alternative Highway Code* offers a useful reminder of the real rules of the road, as well as providing a useful reference point should you suddenly find yourself slowly sinking into a lake in a stupidly-painted VW camper van that you naively believed to be 'watertight'. Either way, the *Top Gear Alternative Highway Code* is an indispensable companion for the modern motoringist. Or, if you're like James May, the old-fashioned motoringist. Please note that earlier versions of this book were erroneously publicised as the *Top Gear Alternative Highway Cod*. Once again, we must stress that this publication has nothing to do with any sort of fish, and that fish enthusiasts should seek out its sister book, *Dynamite Fishing* by J. R. Stigley.

IMPORTANT NOTE:
Due to a series of errors at the conception, writing and production stages, this book does not contain any useful information whatsoever, and should not be used as a guide to either driving OR fish. Sorry.

THE ROAD
A HISTORY

Before we go any further, it's worth taking a moment to look at the history of the British highway in this country. The road was invented in 1919 by Sir Alan Littlechef (later Lord Sideorder of Onionrings) who was seeking a way to attract more customers to his chain of restaurants, which were all situated in the middle of fields. The road was an immediate success and spread rapidly across Great Britain, to the great joy of a population steadily recovering from the Great War and frankly quite sick of having to trudge everywhere through woods, across meadows and along rivers. As with many other great British interwar inventions, such as the ear-hair trimmer and the horse, the road quickly spread across the world and soon became the international standard for getting anywhere, at least until 1974 when Sir Douglas Heathrow-Giftshop invented the aeroplane.

The road continues to this day, but in this modern world the demands on the road are ever greater as an increasing number of things fight for space upon it, including cars, cyclists, motorcyclists, unicyclists, lorry drivers, horse riders, bad pilots and, of course, an escaped leopard.

With this ever-growing demand for road space, it is vital that all road users abide by the same set of clearly defined rules.

THE BASIC RULES OF THE ROAD

HOW TO USE THE ROAD

Using a road is very simple. If you wish to go somewhere, the road should be used in the up-down or vertical orientation.

However, some users may wish to simply 'get over' or 'cross' the road. These users would include:

- pedestrians
- chickens

In such an instance, the road should be used in the left-right or horizontal orientation.

DO NOT attempt to take the road internally. The contents of the road may have settled in transit. **DO NOT** attempt to operate the road when drowsy.

Warning: The road may go up as well as down. These are called 'hills'.

USING THE ROAD IN A CAR

Here are some basic tips for using the road in a car.
Please remember: Many of these rules apply ONLY
to car drivers. Do not attempt to follow them if you
are a pedestrian, a chicken, or an escaped leopard.

BEFORE MOVING OFF YOU SHOULD...

- Get into the car. Always do this BEFORE
  moving off. Trust us, we've tried the other way
  and it ruins your shoes, trousers and face.

- Once in the car, lock the doors really quickly
  but in such a way that passers-by can't see you
  doing it and assume you're a massive coward.

- You are not a massive coward, it's just that you
  know Dave who works in the newsagent, well
  he knew this bloke, yeah, who once got into
  this car and then before he set off, yeah, this
  guy with a knife jumped in the back and
  slashed him, yeah, and then stole all his
  Haribo. Although apparently when the police
  came it turned out it wasn't a bloke with a knife
  at all. It was an escaped leopard.

- Where were we? Oh yeah, next you should
  check your wing-mirrors. Chances are your
  side mirrors are scratched, out of position, held
  on with gaffer tape and connected to the rest
  of the car by a spider's web.

- Switch on the car. Again, it seems quite basic but many people forget. It's worth bearing in mind that forgetting to switch on the engine at the start of a journey can add up to FIVE hours to a journey that would otherwise take 20 minutes, so think on.

- Before pulling away, take time to adjust your radio, air conditioning and (where applicable) testes.

- Rotate your head 180° to check all blind spots are clear. If you cannot rotate your head 180° you should install a Car Owl. Even a standard Car Owl is a valuable safety aid that gives the driver greater awareness of what is around him. Sorry, not Car Owl. We meant 'interior mirror'. There is no such thing as a Car Owl.

- Go, go, go!

PULLING AWAY THE JAMES MAY WAY

- Decide which car you are going to use today.

- Oh dear, you've just remembered that the Rolls is in a garage 20 miles away. That's a bit of an inconvenience.

- Oh blast, it turns out you didn't actually buy that Rover P6 off eBay after all. Must have dreamt that. Make mental note not to keep reading the Rover P6 Haynes manual in bed.

- Decide to take the Fiat Panda.

- Check the tyre pressures, oil level and top up the windscreen-washer fluid.

- Go inside for a nice cup of tea.

- Return to the car and get into it.

- Remove the small, soft-bristled brush from the special brush pouch within the interior tools-storage box.

- Use the small, soft-bristled brush to remove any traces of dust from the dashboard controls and air vents.

- Slip the small, soft-bristled brush back into the special brush pouch and replace it in the interior tools-storage box.

- Ensure all the air vents are lined up.

- Phew, this is thirsty work. Go back inside for a nice cup of tea.

- Return to the car.

- Double-check all the air vents are correctly aligned.

- Turn the ignition to position 1 and assess all gauges and warning lights.

- Oh dear, it seems to have gone dark.

- Depress the clutch and ensure the car is in neutral.

- You are now ready to start the car.

- Ah, hang on. I think the shop might have shut by now. Hmph.

- Go back in the house and have a nice cup of tea. Pop a pie in the oven for dinner. Read Rover P6 Haynes manual in bed.

OVERTAKING

Here is the official Ministry of Top Gear overtaking
procedure, as laid down by the Minister for
Shouting, Lord Clarkson.

- Oh God, there's a Peugeot in the way.

- This is a national-speed-limit road, why is it
  doing 47mph? WHY?

- Ah, there's a straight coming up!

- POWEEEEEEER!

- Ha! This car is BIBLICALLY FAST.

- Knowing look to mini-cam on passenger side.

- Do not try this in a car with ANYTHING less
  than 500 HORSEPOWERS.

OVERTAKING IN A CAR WITH ANYTHING LESS THAN 500 HORSEPOWERS

- Floor the accelerator.

- Feel entire car start to vibrate and rattle like the Space Shuttle on re-entry.

- Feel gentle beads of perspiration gather on whitening knuckles.

- Shout 'Come on, you can do it!'

- Notice huge lorry coming the other way.

- Watch entire life flash before eyes.

- Oh God, why did I accidentally call the teacher 'Mum'?

- Get past dithering Peugeot and pull back to correct side of road.

- Stop to remove mess from underpants.

- Watch Peugeot go past.

- Get savaged by an escaped leopard.

NB: When overtaking, always have a peek at the driver of the vehicle you're passing. We all do it.

TRAFFIC QUEUES

When caught in stationary traffic on your own, the following are recommended ways to pass the time:

- Turn the heater fan on to maximum and watch small pieces of dead leaf getting swirled around at the base of the windscreen.

- Fiddle with the balance controls on the stereo to find out what Chris Evans would sound like if he were in the back seat.

- Yawn.

- Yawn while moving your hand over your mouth to make a Red Indian noise.

- Contemplate sending a text message about the traffic jam to a local radio station travel desk using an 'amusing' nom de plume like

In case of emergency, down contents for a handy receptacle.

I. P. Mypants or S. Piderman but don't because
that's actually as amusing as being crushed by
a falling chest freezer.

- Consider having a wee in an empty Coke
  bottle but think better of it.

- Play five minutes of the audio book you bought
  four years ago before you realised how
  appalling they were.

- Pick at the stain on your jeans and worry what
  caused it.

- Think about Kristin Scott Thomas. Or pasties.
  Or a weird combination of both.

- Invent various ways of executing the massive
  cock who caused this queue.

- Wee into an empty Coke bottle.

When caught in stationary traffic with a passenger, the only reasonable way to pass the time is by playing James May's Dashboard Difference Game.

Here are the rules:
- Player 1 observes the current position of all the buttons, switches and other controls on the car dashboard.
- Player 1 then closes their eyes.
- Player 2 adjusts the position of ONE dashboard button, switch or other control. When this is done they may instruct Player 1 to open their eyes.
- Player 1 then attempts to identify the one button, switch or other control that has been adjusted.
- Repeat.

And if you're bored of that, you could just keep trying to distract your passenger and then turn on their heated seat without them noticing.

ROAD JUNCTIONS

The word junction only applies in the UK. In the US a junction is called an intersection, whereas in Britain Intersection is probably a magazine so trendy that newsagents are expressly forbidden from selling it to you unless you have a violently asymmetric hairstyle.

Popular types of junction include T, Box, and, of course, Clapham. Please note that if you find yourself driving through the latter, something has gone catastrophically wrong and you are about to get hit by a train.

Motorway junctions are unique in that each one bears a number. If you see a numbered junction, that will mean you are on a motorway and not, as you first suspected, on a runway, James. Oh for God's sake, take off or get out of the way!

Give way at road junctions.

Get out of way at railway junctions.

ROUNDABOUTS

There are more than seven roundabouts in Britain, or at least that's what Stig's mate Krell Psistence told us. Mind you, he's the one that's now banned from holding a pub quiz anywhere in Wales as a result of all the consequent violence. Anyway, roundabouts are a vital part of driving, since they ease traffic flow and provide drivers with a handy place in which to have a low-speed accident. Unfortunately, many roundabouts are now broken, the main cause being an old man in a Peugeot who arrived there in 2003 and became so paralysed with fear and confusion that he's still sitting there to this day, blocking one of the entrances with a 217-mile queue behind him.

Avoid 3-hour Mexican stand-offs.

DID YOU KNOW...?

Yellow lines were originally painted with custard.

You should give priority to traffic approaching from your right. Although occasionally two cars will arrive at the same time from opposite directions and then it's time to play roundabout roulette. Each car is on the right-hand side of the other. So who's going to edge out first and who's going to give way? The matter is usually solved with a low-speed accident.

The island at the centre of the roundabout is often sponsored by a local business or organisation. Presumably they have done this because they think it makes them look exciting and dynamic and not, as is actually the case, unimaginative, cheap, and parochial. Do you really want to give your custom to people who concentrate their energies on wooden advertising signs and coloured flowers that spell out the words 'Welcome To Tilehurst'?

MINI-ROUNDABOUTS

Mini-roundabouts are like supply teachers. They're hard to take seriously, no one gives them any respect and they usually end up with tyre marks all over them.

THE RULES FOR
CAR DRIVERS

VEHICLE CONDITION

There are certain basic checks that you should perform on your vehicle before taking to the road. The first of these is to confirm the number of wheels. Here is a handy guide to help you decipher your findings:

NO. OF WHEELS	DIAGNOSIS
One	You have a unicycle. As a result you probably also have some sort of amusing beard and consider yourself 'wacky' even though everyone else thinks you are 'a tit'.
Two	You have a bicycle. Or, if there are two wheels and an engine, a motorbike. Either way, if ceasing to rest your hand on it causes the whole thing to fall over, this is not a car.

THE RULES FOR
CAR DRIVERS

NO. OF WHEELS	DIAGNOSIS
Three	Almost there, but not quite. Technically yes, this might be a car. But it is a car with NOT ENOUGH WHEELS. Also, it's probably a Reliant Robin and you will be forever forced to suffer the embarrassment of having 1980s comedians pointing at you and laughing, while grunting thickos call your car a 'Robin Reliant' even though that's not its name any more than anyone would say, 'Oh look at that saloon car, I think it's a Mondeo Ford.' Idiots. Sorry, where were we? Erm, yes, to sum up: three wheels, not enough.
Four	Yes! Well done. Four wheels mean you have a car. Or two mopeds stapled together. You might want to check that again. Some car dealers are quite unscrupulous.

You should ensure that you throw the unicycle in the canal, set fire to the motorbike or sell the Reliant to a breathlessly giggling Jasper Carrott. Now go and buy a proper car.

Once you have done this you must be sure that it is in a suitable condition to drive on the road. You can do so by asking the following questions:

- Can you see through at least some of the windscreen?

- Is the handbrake strong enough to perform a handbrake turn in order to impress some girls?

- At some point in the last year, did a man in an oily blue overall suck air in through his teeth, tell you that lots of things were wrong with lots of stuff you didn't understand and then charge you £470 to make it all better before giving you a certificate with MOT written on it in Biro?

- Has the escaped leopard been removed from the back seat?

If you can answer 'yes' to all of those questions, you're good to go.

FITNESS TO DRIVE

It is not just your car that must be in a suitable condition for the roads. As a driver, you must be too. You can assess your fitness to drive by asking yourself the following questions:

Can you see?
Do you have at least some arms and legs?
Do you have a driving licence/Are you seriously thinking about getting a driving licence at some point in the future?*
Okay, you're fit to drive. Away you go!

Driving when tired can cause problems. At 70mph on a motorway even the smallest yawn can cause issues such as inattention, loss of control and wasp swallowing. Worse yet, falling asleep at the wheel can lead to severe conditions such as a stiff face, which is a common side effect of smashing into a concrete bridge support. To ensure that you do not become tired at the wheel, here is a handy table:

DO	DO NOT DO
Get a good night's sleep at home.	Get a good night's sleep while travelling at 70mph on the M4.

* Minicab drivers only

Listen to bright, jaunty, up-tempo music.	Listen to Leonard Cohen reciting the Russian dictionary.
Open the window a crack to allow fresh air in.	Light a series of relaxing aromatherapy candles.
Stop at a service area and take a break.	Stop at a service area and have a cocktail of Ovaltine and heroin, all washed down with a delicious Sunday roast followed by apple crumble and custard.
While at the service area buy a take-away coffee for the ongoing journey.	While at the service area buy a duvet and some pillows for the ongoing journey.

VISION

You **MUST** be able to read a vehicle number plate in good light from a distance of 20 metres. If you're doing your driving test, it's easy to get around this bit by memorising all the number plates in the surrounding area. Better still, all number plates ever.

It's worth bearing in mind that if a driving examiner rules that you're basically blind and would be a menace on the road, he is immediately approving you for a job driving a van.

Slow down and if necessary stop if you are dazzled
by sunlight, oncoming headlights, or the light
reflected off Richard Hammond's teeth.

At night or in poor visibility, do not restrict your
vision with tinted glasses, lenses, visors, balaclavas,
welding masks, goggles, microscopes, telescopes,
binoculars or by putting a bag over your head.

BEFORE SETTING OFF ALWAYS REMEMBER THE FOLLOWING TIPS:

- Remember to have a car. It's an easy
  mistake to make. Don't come crying to us
  when you realise it's taken you eight days to
  get from Oxford to Manchester. Of course
  that may NOT be because you're
  accidentally on foot. Sometimes that's the
  normal journey time on the M6.

- Make sure you are sitting in the driving seat and facing the front. You might think this is basic stuff but you'd be amazed how many people in foreign countries insist on sitting on the PASSENGER side of the car, the

bloody idiots. And then they drive on the WRONG side of the road, too. It's an accident waiting to happen.

- Ensure you have planned your route and allowed sufficient time. If you are a wittering simpleton, please allow extra time for following your Sat Nav instructions in an overly literal and pedantic manner that causes you to drive into a canal/shopping centre/live firing-range/any other place

that will generate a newspaper story
specifically formulated so that people can
laugh heartily at your blithering idiocy.

• Make extra sure that you are not a dog. It's
easily done. Yes it is. Yes it IS. Ooo's a good
doggy eh? Ooo is? Yes, oo are. Yes.

VEHICLE TOWING AND LOADING

You should not need to tow anything behind your
car. There is a sound reason for this:

1. If you are towing another car on a trailer, it almost
certainly means it is an old wreck you bought off
eBay when you were drunk. You are now taking it
home where it will sit under a tarpaulin outside
your house for the rest of time, or at least until
your family leave you, possibly with the words
'And you were supposed to move that bloody
"restoration project" THREE YEARS AGO!'

DID YOU KNOW...?

There are such things as GREEN
road markings. They denote a
zone in which you should not stop
to pick up current or previous
members of the Sugababes.

2. If you are towing a caravan you are clearly a wiffling moron with a perverse desire to get in everyone's way until eventually you reach the muddy field next to the diesel locomotive shunting-yard in which you will spend the next two weeks pooing into a bucket like a medieval tramp and sincerely pretending that you are having a good time when in truth, for the price of

your vile fibreglass tomb, you could have bought a fortnight in Barbados and discovered what a good time really feels like.

3. You are towing a horsebox. Again, what is your obsession with getting in the way? Here's the deal – you have a horse. A horse can do something that your car can't. It can go across fields and, with a little encouragement, jump over hedges. So why not use it to do that instead of locking the stupid thing in a small trailer and transporting it by road with a massive train of frustrated cars behind you, all enjoying a magnificent view of an equine's arse?

Ergo, if you are towing anything, stop immediately, disconnect the tow hook and push the trailer down a slope and into a lake. You may first pause to take out the Haynes manual/battered box of Ker-Plunk/ horse if you so wish.

DID YOU KNOW...?

Luxembourg drives on the right- AND the left-hand side of the road. Which side you use is governed by what sort of kitchen you have.

SEAT BELTS AND CHILD RESTRAINTS

- You **MUST** wear a seatbelt in a car, unless it is a minicab and you are the driver, in which case it would be easier to persuade you to use the bloody air-con de-mist setting and not drive everywhere in fifth gear.

- Legally you're supposed to wear a seatbelt if you are a van driver. Legally, no Welshman may enter the City of Chester before sunrise on pain of decapitation, but no one bothers with that legislation either. If they did, Jeremy would have been on the first plane to Chester before you could say 'longbow'.

DRIVERS WHO ARE CARRYING CHILDREN IN CARS, VANS AND OTHER VEHICLES SHOULD ALSO ENSURE THAT:

- Small children are strapped into car seats or booster seats, which takes ages, especially as the buckles are impossible to fit and the fidgety little bastards have been so pumped full of E-numbers they refuse to keep still.
- You have books, toys, games, teddies, music, DVDs, crisps, sweets, fruit, pillows, cushions, favourite blankets, and a lifetime supply of Infacol. Or just some ear plugs and gaffer tape.
- You know at least 16 verses of 'The Wheels On The Bus'.

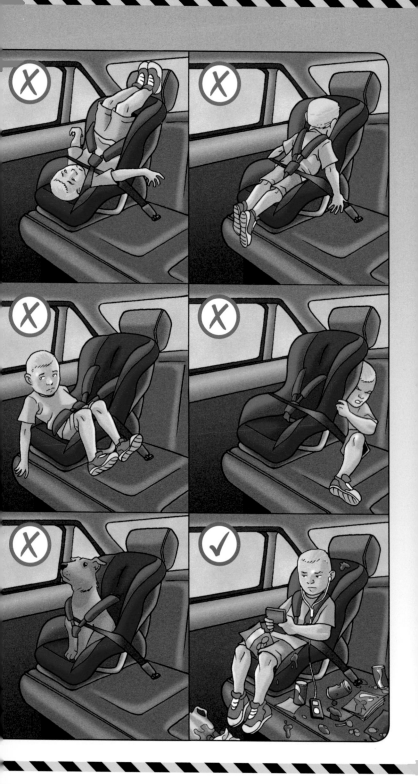

DID YOU KNOW...?

If you reverse fast enough, it's possible to go back in time.

Children should NOT be locked in the boot, attached to the roof rack or dragged from the tow bar, no matter how tempting that is.

SPECIFIC RULES FOR THE STIG

- Stop eating this book.
- Seriously Stig, stop eating it.
- Stig, we won't tell you again!
- Also, let go of the otter!

Always take a snack on long journeys.

THE RULES FOR MOTORCYCLISTS

Motorcycling can be extremely dangerous and extremely stupid. So it's worth following this chapter carefully.

CLOTHING

It is vital to wear the correct protective clothing when motorcycling. Unless by 'motorcycling' you mean 'riding to your job at a media company on your stupid scooter', in which case you believe a T-shirt and ridiculous knee-length trousers will be fine and indeed that you look quite cool, right up until the moment that bits of your body are smeared like pâté across the surface of the road. For proper motorcyclists, a full set of leathers is essential. When selecting your leathers, always choose the set that will most make you look like a slightly camp Power Ranger. If you own a classic motorcycle, you can ignore this advice and choose leathers that help you to resemble the ageing owner of a once-popular fetish club.

PREPARING YOUR MOTORCYCLE

Taking delivery of a new motorcycle is an exciting moment but do not make the mistake of simply jumping on and riding it away as soon as they have unloaded it from the lorry. First you **MUST** rip off the exhaust pipe it was fitted with at the factory and replace it with a large carbon fibre amplifier that will make your new machine sound like a 20-ton wasp trapped inside a chainsaw factory. Once you have done this, you **MUST** then ride up to Jeremy Clarkson's house and spend the afternoon whizzing back and forth along the road outside until he becomes very cross indeed.

DID YOU KNOW...?

If it is not clear who has right of way, the law states that the matter MUST be resolved by raw, ugly violence.

RIDING YOUR MOTORCYCLE

You do not have to ride your motorcycle every day. Instead, you should probably have a car for that. Cars keep you dry in the rain and can stay upright at a standstill without a metal prop on the bottom. However, your motorcycle is the ideal

device to use at a weekend when, like any right-thinking person, all you want to do after a hard week at work is go up to the Peak District and zoom about for no apparent reason before stopping at a pub for a glass of orange juice in the company of fellow balding men in leather clothes.

ORGAN DONOR CARDS

These come as standard with every motorcycle.
Or at least, they probably should.

THE RULES
FOR CYCLISTS

A SHORT HISTORY OF CYCLING

Cycling was invented by the Victorians, purely to give them a distraction while they waited for somebody to come up with the car or, at the very least, a more powerful horse. In 1885 their starchy, moustachioed dreams came true when the Stebbings & Churchmeadow Company of Great Missenden unveiled their new Horse GT, an announcement that was rendered obselete and embarrassing just one hour later when Karl Benz invented the car.

With the invention of the car, and the prototype horse now released from the mechanism, cycling was redundant as a form of transport and reduced to the role of a hobby, specifically for weird families that enjoy dressing up in identical clothes and cheerfully pedalling around the lanes of Suffolk under the mistaken impression that their entire lives must somehow resemble one long yoghurt commercial.

Although in any right-thinking country outside of the Third World cycling should be no more than a pastime, many people in Britain still have a quaint view that it is an acceptable way to commute or to visit the shops. It is, of course, not the role of a Highway Code to judge or belittle these people so instead please observe the following guidelines, written specifically for them:

RULES FOR BITTER LOSERS AND IDIOTS WHO DON'T HAVE CARS

- You **MUST NOT** cycle on a pavement, even though you always do. Equally, pedestrians who spot a cyclist coming along the pavement **MUST NOT** jam an umbrella through one of their wheels.

- You **MUST** assume that somehow you are so special and important that red lights simply do not apply to you. This is fair enough. Although please bear in mind that if you're going to be such an arrogant little prick you should understand that ambulances and A&E departments do not apply to you either.

- You **MUST** get into a ludicrously self-righteous argument with a bus driver, signally failing to notice that a) he really doesn't give a flying fart whose right of way it was, and b) he has control of a 10-ton twat-crusher.

- You **MUST** weave through stationary traffic with an air of quite incredible smugness, even though you're the one that will arrive at work drenched in sweat and lorry-drivers' mucus.

- Cycle couriers: You **MUST** behave like an unbelievable cock-end. Oh wait, you already do.

You **MUST** wear the correct gear. You know – the stuff that makes you look like an extra from a gay rave video. Tight Lycra, girlie backpack, brain-squeezing baseball cap, elaborate water bottle that looks like it was designed for the International Space Station and not the inside lane of the A414.

ADDITIONAL GUIDANCE FOR 'SEMI-PRO' SUNDAY CYCLISTS

You know the ones. Middle-aged and either ruddy faced and overweight like a heart attack waiting to happen, or extremely thin and overly wiry like a piece of gristle wrapped in Lycra. Either way, they've probably shaved their legs, claiming that 'it's easier to put a plaster on them when you fall off and graze yourself'. This is rubbish. They shave their legs because they like it.

Please observe the following guidelines, you smooth-shinned perverts:

- Ensure you go just fast enough to keep a car stuck behind you, but slow enough to be really annoying.
- On tight, twisty country lanes, ride three abreast and chat to one another, carefully ignoring the vehicle that's weaving around behind you with a steam cloud of pure rage fizzing from the windows.
- Wherever possible, arrange races for bang in the middle of a Sunday when you can cause the most disruption, perhaps based on the false assumption that everyone actually wants to see your big, fat, lobster-red, sweaty faces.

YOU AND YOUR BICYCLE

Cyclists should be confident of their ability to ride on the road without getting in the way and being a massive tit. Be sure that:

- Your bike is not a girl's bike (unless you are a girl).

- Your wheels do not have Spokey Dokes (unless you are a 14-year-old boy from 1982).

- Your brakes work and you know how to use them (you'll be surprised how often this isn't the case).

- You can get on and off the bike without giving yourself a hernia or creating an embarrassing rip in your trousers.

It is recommended that you fit a bell to your bicycle because this makes you look even more ridiculous. There's few funnier things in life than the sight and sound of a peeved cyclist ineffectually ringing their teensy-weensy bell at a speeding 12-ton juggernaut. Yes, my trouser-clipped friend – he won't mess with you again. Mainly because he's made a mess of the tarmac with the remains of your head.

THE RULES FOR CYCLISTS

THE RULES FOR
PEDESTRIANS

There is no point walking. Walking is something you do to get from the sofa to the refrigerator in order to fetch a nice snack just before something good comes on the television. Walking is not a way to move around outside of your house. What you need to do is buy a car. A car will get there ten times quicker and you won't be covered in rain. Plus you get to sit down.

GENERAL GUIDANCE

- If you must walk, keep to the pavement. That's the deal; you get the pavement, drivers get the road.

- When using the pavement, walk as far away from the kerb as possible, preferably right up against the wall. That way you'll spare drivers the sight of your miserable, tired face.

- If there is no pavement, keep to the right-hand side of the road. But don't get cocky. Remember, you're a guest, okay?

- Help other road users to see you. When it is dark, wear light-coloured clothes, reflective armbands, sashes and fluorescent waistcoats. This will make you more visible to traffic. What's more, it'll give them a good laugh at your expense.

PARKED VEHICLES

Never cross the road in front of, or behind, any vehicle with its engine running. Unless you're that baldy man from R.E.M. in the video for 'Everybody Hurts'. The bit when everyone climbs onto the roof of their cars is quite good, actually. But you probably shouldn't try it if you live in Shrewsbury.

REVERSING VEHICLES

Never cross behind a vehicle that is reversing. Especially lorries that have a voice repeating the phrase: 'Warning! Vehicle reversing!' Note to pedestrians in southwest England; this voice isn't a ghost, a robot, black magic, or the captured soul of a dead ancestor. It's a recording. A re-cor-ding. Look, don't worry about that now, we'll come back to it in another publication.

MOVING VEHICLES

You **MUST NOT** get on to a moving vehicle or hold on to a moving vehicle. You are not in *Back To The Future*. Time travel is not possible; if it were, the present would be full of visitors from the future and Jeremy would be constantly popping back to 1976 in order to buy more records and clothes.

PELICAN CROSSINGS

These are signal-controlled crossings operated by pedestrians. (Actually, they're not. The button doesn't really work. It's not connected to a wire or anything. It's just there to give pedestrians something to do while they're waiting and to give them a false sense of self-importance. Don't tell them though. Keep the stupid, button-pressing monkeys in their ignorance.)

Red Man –
Do Not Cross. Unless you reckon you can get away with it. Go on – run! RUN LIKE THE WIND!

Green Man –
Cross With Care. Take your time. Enjoy yourself. Why not stop halfway and do a little dance. DANCE, MONKEY BOY, DANCE!

Flashing Green Man – Do Not Start To Cross. Unless there's an old lady halfway across – she's like the 'buffer' that will stop you getting run over. Ha! THE WEAK WILL PERISH!

THE RULES FOR PEDESTRIANS

PUFFIN CROSSINGS

These are like a pelican crossing but, er, smaller. And, oh I don't know, they use less fish.

TOUCAN CROSSINGS

Yes, there really is something called a toucan crossing. It's something to do with a crossing that allows pedestrians and cyclists to share the same space. Because, of course, cyclists would never normally ride roughshod across areas that are meant to be used only by pedestrians, oh dearie me, no.

EQUESTRIAN CROSSINGS

Yes, these really do exist. Although no one has ever seen one. It is almost certainly a front for some massive expenses scam within the Department of Transport. 'That's right, Minister – we need £400m to install, er… equestrian crossings throughout central London. Actually, can you make the cheque payable to me…?'

DUCK-BILLED PLATYPUS CROSSINGS

Ah, now these definitely don't exist. Which is a shame. They'd be really funny.

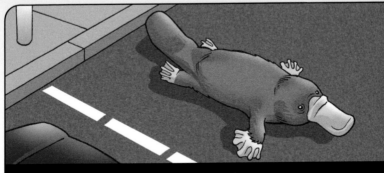

Beware of animals made out of spare parts.

SITUATIONS NEEDING EXTRA CARE

EMERGENCY VEHICLES

If an ambulance, fire engine, police or other emergency vehicle approaches using flashing blue lights, headlights and/or sirens, keep off the road. There's a chance you'll end up in some dreadful satellite TV show presented by that bloke who used to read the news.

And definitely do not chase after an emergency vehicle unless you're a lawyer for some crappy website like BlameSomeoneElseDirect.com and you reckon you can make a few quid out of someone's tragic misfortune. Or help them to consolidate all of their accidents into one big, easy-to-manage accident. The kind that will help them to use their blithering stupidity to ultimately make your car insurance renewal so massive you'll have to pay it in liquid gold and unicorn pieces.

DID YOU KNOW...?

It's illegal to sleep, send text messages, or play table tennis while driving.

BUSES

Be especially cautious when getting on/off a bus. This is a high-risk situation that presents risks such as unprovoked knife frenzy, escaped leopard attack, and being seen by people you know as they drive past in their cars. You might also trip over an old lady and her massive tartan shopping trolley full of cat food, tinned beetroot and pre-packaged five-day-long anecdotes about rationing.

Avoid violent predators (and escaped leopards).

THE RULES
ABOUT
ANIMALS

GENERAL GUIDANCE

It is ILLEGAL for the following animals to drive a car*.

Badger	**Honey Badger**	**Weasel**	**Cheese Weasel**
Weasel 1.6 GLX	**Other weasels and weasel derivatives**	**Dog**	**Dog disguised as Zebra**
Talking Crow	**Alan the Hamster**	**The Helena Staples Ant Ensemble**	**Bugs Bunny (after the drink-driving ban)**

* An earlier version of the *Top Gear Alternative Highway Code* may have erroneously included 'Michael Schumacher' in the list of things that can't drive. We now accept that this is wholly wrong and apologise for any distress caused. The entry should of course have read 'Ralf Schumacher'.

It is LEGAL for the following animals to drive a car (probably).

Trevor the Trained Monkey.

HORSES

Horses are bastards. Unfortunately they have some pretty powerful friends in Westminster and, even though they are literally the most stupid animals in the world and get freaked out by an old carrier bag snagged on a hedge or the sight of their own reflection in a puddle, they are somehow allowed to use the roads, alongside cars and vans and other more reasonable ways to get around that don't leave a massive pile of turds just to the left of the white line.

If you insist on riding a horse, you must use a bridleway where possible. You **MUST NOT** take a horse onto a footpath or pavement, onto a cycle track, into a shopping centre, onto a moving escalator, up a stepladder or to Paris on a weekend for two by Eurostar.

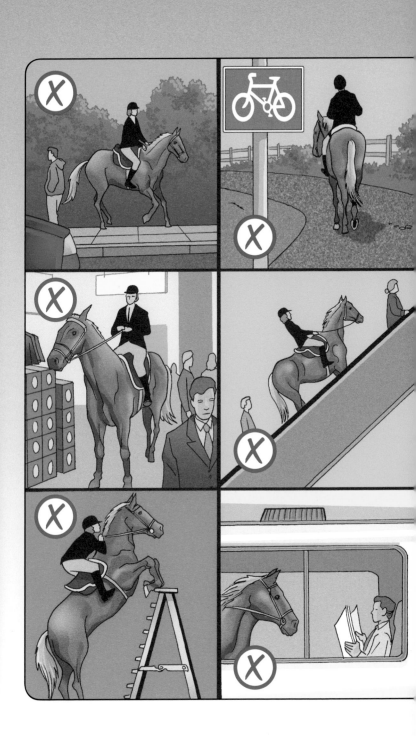

OTHER ANIMALS

When in a vehicle, make sure dogs or other animals are suitably restrained so they cannot attack you while you are driving. Do not let your animal drive the vehicle even if it claims to have only had one glass of wine and to feel 'fine'.

A seat-belt harness, pet carrier, dog cage or dog guard are ways of restraining animals in cars. But a sack and a piece of rope are much quicker and cheaper.

DID YOU KNOW...?

Statistically the safest drivers are Dutch lesbian loss adjusters in a blue car near Ipswich.

ANIMALS & THE ROAD

- If your vehicle hits an animal, pull to a controlled halt, inspect the damage, and shout 'Yes! 20 Points!'
- If you hit an elephant, you are either extremely unlucky or about to be sacked as a zookeeper.
- Hitting an animal can be a distressing experience. Especially if it has scratched the bit you only had re-sprayed last year.
- If the animal is still alive, call a vet and ask for help.
- If the animal is dead, call Hugh Fearnley-Whittingstall and ask for a recipe.

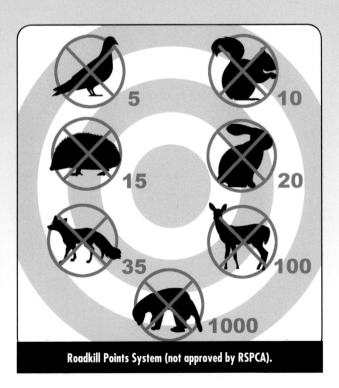

Roadkill Points System (not approved by RSPCA).

ADDITIONAL RULES AND GUIDANCE

MOTORWAYS

Motorways are the Jeremy Clarksons of the road network. Compared to other roads, they are bigger, faster, noisier, and they are going bald. Actually, that probably only applies to actual Jeremy and not the tenuous-analogy Jeremy we're talking about here. Anyway, here are some rules and hints for motorway driving:

When driving in the outside lane, always ensure you throw the following items onto the central reservation:

- Single shoe.
- Hub cap.
- Smashed wing mirror.
- Unidentified section of bumper.
- Plastic bag.
- 47 yards of cassette tape.

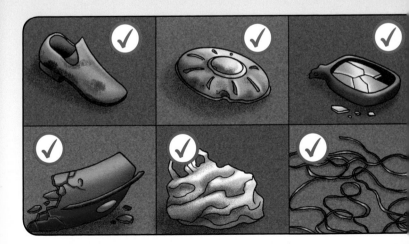

If you are using the motorway to get to a football match, always ensure that you have a team scarf shut in one of your windows so that it can flutter in the breeze and allow fans of rival teams to gob on you as they pass. You may also find it helpful to fit the back seat of your car with a fat bloke in a comically terrible team hat who is busily stuffing a pasty into his face.

Coach drivers should ensure their passengers look as depressed as possible, staring vacantly out of the window and wishing they had enough money for a train or, failing that, a decent suicide.

Be aware of slow-moving traffic joining from the slip road, long vehicles, and cars suddenly slamming on the brakes because they think they're passing a police car only to realise it's the Traffic Wombles in their Highways Agency car and they can't do jack shit.

Please remember that what the Traffic Wombles CAN do is exorcise all their inherent petty-minded bitterness and all those years of being bullied at school by closing an entire motorway just because someone's door mirror has fallen off. It's worth bearing that terrifying prospect in mind when you find yourself repeatedly unable to get home in time to see your children and are then forced to hear the tales of their sad slide into prostitution and heroin addiction from your wife, and realise that the entire break-up of your family and your own personal slide into alcoholism and ultimately homelessness was originally caused almost entirely by a self-righteous Brummie with a moustache and a Health & Safety certificate who decided he was going to make thousands of people late all because he had been given road-closing powers that made him feel better about the basic failure of his own miserable, inadequate life.

When passing speed cameras, do observe the speed limit, even though you're pretty damn sure they don't work and it's just a scare tactic, a bit like TV detector vans and the Liberal Democrats.

On a two-lane motorway or an A-road, lorry drivers should always ensure they begin an overtaking manoeuvre at the bottom of a really steep hill, as if they've absent-mindedly forgotten that they're in 44 tons of articulated leviathan and are idly thinking, 'Golly, my Lotus feels a bit sluggish today…'

Remember: The hard shoulder is reserved for emergencies. Namely, small children having a pee against the verge while their parents skulk around trying to avoid eye contact with passing traffic.

Motorway service stations should only used in emergencies. That is – when you're about to wet yourself. Be aware of the following hazards:

- The bored bloke from the motoring organisation standing by the entrance. No, I DO NOT want to join the AA. Although actually, if you said yes he wouldn't have the faintest idea what to do because no one's ever talked to him before. He'd probably panic, give you a complimentary Biro and then run into a hedge.
- The video games arcade. It hasn't been vacuumed since 1976, and if you stand still

for more than six seconds they have to send in the fire brigade to cut you free.

- The men from a stag weekend all dressed as pirates. Mmm, that's as funny as Ebola in an orphanage.
- THREE QUID for a bag of sweets? Jee-sus!
- Coach parties. A contradiction in terms, like 'Fun Run' and 'Military Intelligence'. Although in the 1970s, people used to have 'coach parties' in their houses. You just got 40 friends over to sit in a tightly confined space that smelt of stale fruit and urine, then got five Glaswegian squaddies to rampage about spraying everything with lager until you wanted to stab yourself with the straw from your box of Kia-Ora.

COUNTRY ROADS

Take extra care on country roads. Especially as the locals will be surprised to see horseless carriages made of metal. Be prepared for pedestrians, cyclists, horse-riders, slow-moving farm machinery, inbred families, endless swathes of mud, racism, a complete loss of mobile phone signal, pubs where the same lonely blokes sit in the same seats every single night of the week, posh people with double-barrelled names, poor people with double-barrelled shot guns, 4x4s driven by clueless berks in Barbour jackets, Bill Oddie, Guy Ritchie, the cast of *Last of the Summer Wine* and the overpowering stench of cow excrement being put through the letter box of your second home.

SINGLE-TRACK ROADS

These are about as much fun as ice cream laced
with razor blades. Driving on a single-track road
means getting lost, getting stuck, getting caught
behind a tractor and getting your car smeared
in crap. Inevitably, you'll meet a massive 4x4
coming the other way that will either force you onto
a verge before thundering past at 60mph because
it's driven by a maniac or crawl past at 2mph
because it's driven by a chinless wonder who can't
gauge the car's width or comprehend that a 4x4 is
actually designed to drive through mud.

DRIVING IN ADVERSE CONDITIONS

WET WEATHER

If it rains, you do two things. Firstly, put your wipers
on. And secondly, don't drive like a twat and crash
into someone else. Oh, and thirdly, appreciate that
you're getting your car washed for free rather than
giving three eastern European men a fiver to do it
in the forecourt of an abandoned petrol station.

Take extra care when overtaking lorries. They make
a lot of spray, even with those doormat things taped
to the mud flaps. F1 drivers always say racing in
the wet is like 'overtaking a lorry in the rain with no
wipers'. Well, boo-hoo! You're still getting
£200,000 for 90 minutes work, plus you get to go
back to your yacht for an all-you-can-eat buffet of
roast swan and Brazilian flange.

DID YOU KNOW...?

You can be fined for driving with an inappropriate hairstyle.

MOIST WEATHER

There is no such thing as 'moist weather'. That faintly odd man off BBC weather does not come on and say 'tomorrow it's going to be... moist'. The only time you'll hear 'moist' spoken in relation to prevailing conditions is when Jeremy uses it to describe a lap by a star in the Reasonably Priced Car that was performed on a damp track, and usually he's just doing it because the guest is a girl and he's trying to be flirtatious.

SNOW

The biggest hazard when driving in snow is that you have to listen to the travel reports on the radio with their constant obsession with TRAVEL CHAOS! This is a particular risk if you are congenitally allergic to being given advice so patronising that it makes your teeth tingle. Examples of this advice may include 'Do not make any journey unless absolutely necessary!' – a slice of mindlessly banal noise that somehow presumes our roads are typically full of people who have nothing to do all day except drive around for the sheer hell of it.

ADDITIONAL RULES AND GUIDANCE

'Goodbye dear, I'm just off to drive to Chichester and back for no earthly reason!' The other hazard during snow is ringing a friend in Sweden or Canada and being forced to listen to them laughing themselves dizzy for 20 minutes at Britain's pathetically inept attempts to maintain a transport infrastructure in the face of one medium-sized snowflake.

WINDY WEATHER

Strong gusts can blow a car, lorry, cyclist or motorcyclist off course. Beware of sudden twitches, unexpected winds and loss of control. Stop giggling. This is not a fart gag.

FOG

In the past it was literally impossible for motorists to tell when it was foggy. At least, we must assume so because what other reason could the authorities possibly have for installing those expensive dot matrix signs on motorways that can flash up the word FOG when we've already been driving through the stuff for the past 15 minutes? Surely it can't just be because they're a bunch of patronising morons wasting all our time and money? If you're interested, there is a difference between fog, smog, mist and low cloud. Unfortunately, only weather people know what it is and they're refusing to say. Although Dave who works in the newsagent reckons it's something to do with geese.

LIZARD ATTACK

There is no such thing as lizard attack.

Lizard attacks (probably) won't happen.

WAITING AND PARKING

PARKING

You **MUST NOT** stop or park:

- On the carriageway or hard shoulder of a motorway except in an emergency.

- On double yellow lines unless you've put your hazards on and are just using the cash machine.

- On a pedestrian crossing.

- On a railway crossing.

- Underwater.

- In a tree.

- Inside an industrial car-crusher.

- Near monkeys.

- On the runway of Norwich International Airport.

- In Queen Beatrix of Denmark's bedroom.

- In Queen Beatrix of Denmark's kitchen.

- In Queen Beatrix of Denmark's hat vestibule.

- In Queen Beatrix of Denmark's amphitheatre of cheeses.

- In Queen Beatrix of Denmark.

- On top of Mick Hucknall (except in an emergency).

DID YOU KNOW...?

Traffic lights used to have four colours – red, amber, green and terracotta cream with a hint of cyan. The latter was used for decorators and gay men.

PARKING THE STIG WAY

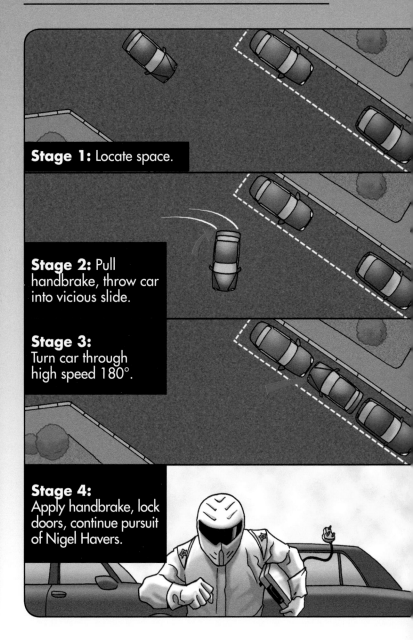

Stage 1: Locate space.

Stage 2: Pull handbrake, throw car into vicious slide.

Stage 3: Turn car through high speed 180°.

Stage 4: Apply handbrake, lock doors, continue pursuit of Nigel Havers.

MANOEUVRING

TURNING IN THE ROAD USING FORWARD AND REVERSE GEARS

That's right. It used to be called a three-point turn. Then some people in Swansea had A LOT of meetings about it, and now it's not called that any more. Anyway, here goes:

- Pull in to the left-hand side of the road.

- Check that there is no traffic coming in either direction.

- Pull forwards and apply full right-hand steering lock.

- Sorry, can we just check – are you reading this while attempting a three-point turn?

- If you ARE reading this while performing a three-point turn, slowly apply the handbrake, put the car into neutral, turn off the engine, get out of the car and walk steadily away from it. Keep walking and never go back. Sorry, but some people just

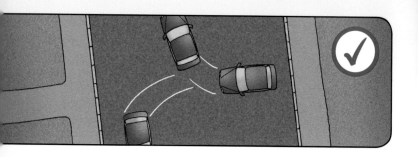

aren't meant to do certain things. Jeremy and football, for example. Or Richard and football. Or James and football. That's why there is no *Top Gear* presenters' five-a-side team. Well, that, and the fact that they're two people short, which wouldn't happen if Chris Goffey and William Woollard didn't always claim to be 'busy' whenever we've got the leisure centre booked. Where were we? Oh yes, please don't take this personally, but if you need a book to talk you through doing a three-point turn then you simply should not be driving, ever. Now go away.

TURNING IN THE ROAD USING THE FORWARD AND REVERSE GEARS WHEN DRIVING A LIMOUSINE YOU'VE MADE YOURSELF OUT OF AN OLD FIAT PANDA, YOU BIG IDIOT!

•   Pull in to the left-hand side of the road.

•   Check that there is no traffic coming in either direction.

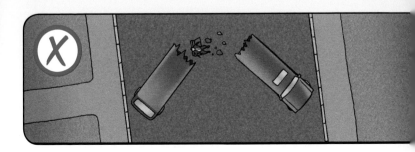

- Pull forwards and... oh dear, what was that grinding noise?

- Pull forwards and apply full right-hand steering lock.

- Ignore the underwhelmed cries of a distant Chris Moyles.

- Ah, that's not really enough lock.

- Engage reverse... sorry, it always does that!

- Reverse while applying full left-hand lock... what was that bang?

- Ask Chris Moyles to confirm that the bollard could probably be glued back together.

- Drive forward while applying full right-hand lock.

- Ignore the motorists who are now being held up by a massive tube of Fiat Panda-shaped nuisance.

- Reverse while applying full... oh God, not the same bollard again!

- Ah yes, that man in the blue Focus seems to be VERY angry now.

- Move forwards while applying... look, I'm doing the best I can! Yes, that's right, madam, it's him off the radio...

- Reverse while… it's jammed under the car now? Oh God!

- Move forwards while… what was that noise? No, the other noise. The sort of creaking one…

- Entire car snaps in half.

- Damn!

DID YOU KNOW...?

Recent research into edible tyres has been cancelled after scientists realised the idea was 'unhygienic and silly'.

RULES FOR AMPHIBIOUS CARS (THAT YOU'VE MADE IN A SHED)

Before using any amphibious car you should first ensure that you are confident of your nautical knowledge. By which we mean you have either watched *The Hunt For Red October* and *Speed 2: Cruise Control* (Jeremy), once opened a supermarket in Southampton (Richard), or taken the trouble to find out what a 'bosun' is (James).

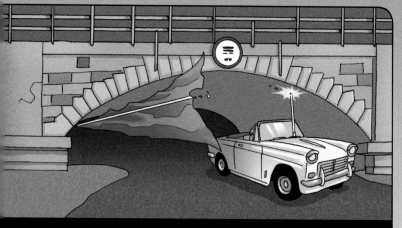
Quick way to lower mast.

When using an amphibious car on the road, normal road rules apply just as they would for any car. The only difference being that you should avoid low bridges if, for some blitheringly stupid reason, you've fitted your craft with an enormous mast.

Upon entering the water, different rules will apply to your vehicle. For example, if your amphibious craft is a VW camper van made to look like a canal boat, you should enter the water, immediately discover that your design doesn't work and then sink rapidly to the bottom of the lake or sea having travelled the sum total of no more than 17 feet. Mostly downwards.

If your craft is fitted with a mast, please remember to let the boom of the mast strike you about the head and face at least 15 times as you bimble

ADDITIONAL RULES
AND GUIDANCE

78 RULES FOR AMPHIBIOUS CARS

Quick way to lower self-esteem.

about before colliding with some reeds/canoeists/ cross-channel container ships. Then sink.

If your amphibious car is some sort of pick-up truck crudely stuffed with expanding foam and then foolishly equipped with a massive outboard motor in the mistaken belief that POWEEER!! can batter anything out of the way, even enormous bodies of water up to and including the English Channel, it turns out you might be right. But only on the second attempt. Please remember that on your first attempt, as your craft turns the wrong way up, you should flail around like a greased seal in a life vest.

Finally, please try not to say 'How hard can it be?' in a strident voice. As soon as you do that it means something bad is going to happen and you may as well have shouted 'Hey everyone, WATCH ME DROWN!'

ADDITIONAL RULES
AND GUIDANCE

RULES FOR CLASSIC CARS

When driving a classic car you should make allowances for the different ways in which an older design can react to such basics as braking, steering, accelerating and, of course, having a curly-haired buffoon behind the wheel shouting 'COME ON! WORK, DAMN YOU, WORK!'

While driving a classic car, bear in mind that the producers only gave you £500 to buy it and you thought you were being clever by keeping back £350 of that in order to use it later on when you decide to fit massive wheels/a spoiler of a Boeing/ flames painted up the sides.

Always remember that an older car may not be as reliable as a new car, especially if you've already tried to lap the *Top Gear* test track in it and funny green stuff started coming out of the bottom. In the event of a breakdown, try to coast to a halt in either a) a place where the cameras can see you or b) a hedge.

If you see a fellow classic-car driver who has broken down, it is common courtesy to stop and ascertain exactly what the problem is. Then speed off, shouting 'LOOOO-SER!' while James stands there in the rain and clouds of steam looking like a drowned and thoroughly depressed spaniel.

ROAD USERS REQUIRING EXTRA CARE

Some road users require that you pay extra care and attention when in their vicinity. These will typically be road users who are confused, disorientated and afflicted with poor reactions and/or vision. Although it can be difficult to identify these high-risk road users from a distance, they do carry an identifying mark that can be easily read from a reasonable distance. The identifying mark for these slow-moving and erratically incompetent road users is as follows:

• Peugeot.

DID YOU KNOW...?

Between 1994 and 2002 a typing error in US legislation meant that anyone over the age of 80 had to re-take a diving test.

ADDITIONAL RULES AND GUIDANCE

LANE-HOGGERS

Yes, you've got a BMW X5. Well done. When you get home, why not have another look at the paperwork that came with it. Can you see the paragraph that says 'Congratulations! Not only do you now have a car that makes you look like a spoon-faced minor-league footballer or cocaine dealer, but also you are now the legal owner of the outside lane of the M6 and you can sit in it all day long, even if the other two lanes are completely clear!' Have you found that paragraph in the paperwork yet? Have you? No. Because it DOES NOT EXIST! Now MOVE OVER!

G-WIZZERS

Make way for Noddy! It's an eco-penis in a car that wouldn't need its batteries and electric motors if

DID YOU KNOW...?

It is very hard to drive in Belarus because, although the country contains over 10,000 cars, roads are illegal!

only they could find a way to harness the raw power of smugness. This is fine; you've bought your snake oil and that was your decision, but could you find a way to get from your office to wherever it is in Islington or Notting Hill that you live that doesn't involve getting in everyone else's way as your grim plastic box struggles to whine its way up an incline so shallow even water could run up it? Oh, and it's all very well thinking you're saving the world, but have you seen those G-Wiz crash tests? Yes, the planet might be about to die, but if you keep driving that volt-sucking coffin, SO ARE YOU!

AUDI TDIERS

Doing well at work, are we? Good mates with the fleet manager, are we? Somehow managed to avoid being given another Passat, did we? Oh yes, you've got an AUDI now. And it's the TDI. Mmm, lots of torques for you! Never mind that everyone knows it's just a VW in a posh suit; you can still leave that four-ringed key on the table in Platinum or whatever other sorry sweat palace of a nightclub you frequent and everyone will be reeeeally impressed. That's all okay. Frankly, the way you live your dismal, new-build-apartment life is up to you. But just remember that the safe distance between you and the car in front on a motorway is not, and never has been, ONE SODDING MILLIMETRE! Now BACK OFF!

ADDITIONAL RULES
AND GUIDANCE

DRIVING OVERSEAS

Many foreign countries insist on driving on the wrong side of the road like big silly idiots. In the circumstances, it is probably best not to make any attempt to 'convert' them to the 'correct' way of thinking. Rather, you should simply go along with their silly ideas. Otherwise, you will probably end up in one of their silly hospitals.

AIRBORNE CARAVANNING

If you have just turned your caravan into an airship, the first thing to consider is what the hell is wrong with you? Seriously, did you really think that was a good idea? Really? Fine.

Assuming your caravan airship gets off the ground, it is always advisable to map out the route that your craft will take. You can do this by getting a normal map and asking a two year old to scribble a continuous line around it.

DID YOU KNOW...?

If all the roads in the UK were laid end-to-end, it would make it extremely hard to get to Wales.

When considering any route, always ensure that you have included a small detour across an international airport, even if it's just a fairly rubbish one like Norwich.

Finally, once you have landed your caravan airship – probably sideways and a bit upside-down – always remember to batten down the hatches for a subsequent burst of righteous indignation from the *Daily Mail* as they attempt to claim that your entire flight was 'YET ANOTHER EXAMPLE OF BBC FAKERY!'

RULES FOR USERS OF POWERED WHEELCHAIRS AND POWERED MOBILITY SCOOTERS

Mobility scooters are an excellent way for the elderly to get confused and accidentally drive onto the hard shoulder of a motorway, allowing them to be spotted by a CCTV camera and the image from that camera to be used in an amusing tabloid newspaper story.

ADDITIONAL RULES AND GUIDANCE

DID YOU KNOW...?

I am living a lie and want to be a woman.

RULES FOR TAXI DRIVERS

The rules of the road are strictly governed and must be observed to ensure safe driving. However, taxi drivers have a God-given right to ignore them. After all, they know everything there is to know about driving, road manners and everything else. Thankfully, they're keen to pass on that information to their clients, other road users, and radio phone-ins (simply by shouting at the radio).

Minicab drivers are granted certain exceptions: insurance, MOT, and a driver's licence.

Traffic lights are purely optional. Examine the passing traffic – then chance it.

RULES FOR ELDERLY DRIVERS

Maintain a speed at least 20mph below the maximum speed limit.

Indicate at least 500 metres before turning. And then change your mind at the last minute.

ADDITIONAL RULES
AND GUIDANCE

Try not to change gear more than once every 15 minutes, because it 'wastes petrol' and 'damages the engine'.

Use Sundays for sightseeing trips on tight country lanes. The most common sight will be a tailback of furious drivers attempting to get past you.

Repeatedly say to your spouse 'I don't know why he's flashing me. I'm doing 23 as it is. This chap's a maniac!'

When a car approaches on the opposite side of the road, apply brakes and slow to a virtual halt.

Do not use the motorway hard shoulder for emergencies. Instead, use it for picnics and photo opportunities.

Repeat the phrase 'Fifty-six years I've been driving and never had a single accident'. Even though you've probably caused half a dozen.

RULES FOR BUS DRIVERS

As a bus driver, your sole purpose in life is to be an irritation to your customers, your fellow road users, and all mankind. There's only one person lower down the evolutionary scale than a bus driver. And that's a bus passenger.

'I look down on him, because I'm a bus driver.' 'I know my place.'

Cyclists should be respected and given a wide berth when overtaken. And when we say 'wide', we mean considerably more than 2.7 millimetres.

When you see someone running for the bus, wait until the last possible moment before shutting the door in their face and pulling away. This ensures maximum frustration for the aspiring passenger and maximum twattery for yourself.

When the lower deck of the bus is busy and people are waiting to get on, don't ask people to move upstairs. Simply sit stationary, keep the front door shut and refuse to let people on.

Every now and again, make sure yourself or a colleague removes the entire top deck of a double-decker bus by ramming it headfirst into a low bridge. The classic excuse 'I forgot' is always guaranteed to raise a tabloid headline and a hearty chuckle. Swiftly followed by the horrific realisation that any day soon you'll most likely be decapitated as a result of an absent-minded bus driver.

DID YOU KNOW...?

Contrary to popular belief, there is no such thing as the M4.

SPEED CAMERAS

Speed cameras are designed to slow down traffic. Which they do for all of 3.2 seconds when you spot the stupid yellow box, brake furiously just before the lines begin, then accelerate away the moment they finish.

Occasionally all drivers suffer 'Flash Paranoia'. This is when a speed camera flashes in your vicinity

ADDITIONAL RULES AND GUIDANCE

even though you're pretty sure it wasn't you breaking the limit. Although, it might have been... I mean, you do tend to leave it late... and you've had a couple of lucky escapes in the past... . You now have no alternative but to cross your fingers and wait two weeks for something to come through the post. Curse you, world! Curse you, Maurice Gatsonides, perfidious Dutch inventor of the Gatso! Why is life so cruel? Then again, it could have flashed for the BMW X5 that was coming the other way, in which case the smug little bastard deserves everything he gets.

Speed cameras prevent accidents (except the ones involving speed cameras).

TRAFFIC CALMING

Some roads have special features such as road humps, chicanes, and narrowings. These are described as 'Traffic Calming' measures. A more accurate title would be 'Driver Baiting' measures. Yes, road humps do slow down your vehicle, but only by knackering your suspension, deflating your tyres, and forcing you to drive halfway across the road to hit the gap properly.

There are two schools of thought when it comes to speed bumps. One is to slow down and place your car in the centre of the road with your tyres either side in order to straddle the bump and minimise disruption to the ride height. The second strategy is to keep your foot down, hit the bump head on, and enjoy a short jump through the air like a post-accident Eddie Kidd or some low-budget edition of *The Dukes of Hazzard*.* Again, this will knacker your car but at least you'll have fun along the way.

Road humps are sometimes referred to as 'sleeping policemen'. This derives from an early example of traffic calming in which policemen would attempt to deter speeding drivers by lying in the road, pulling out a pillow and bedding down for the night. It would work extremely effectively the first time, and reasonably well thereafter, as drivers slowed to avoid the bloody remains of a crushed, misguided constable. Best described as a 'Pyrrhic Victory'.

* *The Dukes of Hazzard* was pretty low budget to start with. As far as we can tell, no money was spent on the script, the acting, or Daisy Duke's costume.

TRAMWAYS

Don't drive on a tramway, don't park on a tramway, don't block a tramway. That's about it, really. Let's face it – how many times do you come across a tramway?

DID YOU KNOW...?

Just because you have an Audi A3 TDI does not mean you HAVE to drive like a total anus.

ROAD WORKS

Road works are carried out by the Highways Agency to benefit road users and reduce journey times, but mainly to bolster Britain's traffic-cone industry.

When encountering road works, stay in lane, slow to a safe speed and pray you'll emerge this side of Christmas.

If the road works are taking place at Christmas, pray you'll emerge this side of eternity.

It is recommended that you make a sarcastic comment about 'road workers' being a contradiction in terms.

Be extra careful when passing a line of traffic cones in case a student decides to put one on his head, or mime licking a giant ice cream.

Look out for overhead signs that warn of road works just after you pass the last available exit and enter a 10-mile tail back.

To the untrained eye, road works can look amateur and disorganised. That is because they are.

If directed to use the hard shoulder, think twice. It might seem fun, but most of them are covered in crap and you'll have to suffer close-up views of children weeing into the verge.

Beware bad student humour.

Major road works **MUST** carry an estimated completion date that is laughably ambitious and usually six months out of date.

To calculate the correct completion date, add twelve months, add another twelve months, add the amount of time it would take for you to do it with a trowel and a bucket of cement, and then double it. You're about halfway there.

In the case of motorway maintenance, a lane will close at least three miles before the first sign of activity. This activity will usually consist of three men standing around a clapped-out stream roller while taking turns to hold a spade.

When approaching road works, drivers **MUST** repeat the phrase 'I can't believe they *still* haven't finished this'.

When passing road works, drivers **MUST** repeat the phrase 'Look, there's no one even there!'

When leaving road works, drivers **MUST** repeat the phrase 'It's outrageous. What are we paying them for?'

Be extra careful to look out for cranes, dumper trucks, diggers, and pneumatic drills. Even though you're a fully-grown adult, there's still a part of you that wishes you had one.

Heavy machinery is cool.

Should it be necessary for two lanes to merge into one, drivers should observe the 'zip method' – so called because some twit always attempts to skip a turn and zip in front of you.

If directed to use a contraflow system, keep to the speed limit and watch in impotent rage as the traffic in the inside lane proceeds at twice the speed of yours.

When leaving road works and resuming the national speed limit, take extra effort to squeeze the accelerator so you hit the new speed limit at exactly the same moment as you pass the sign. This is immensely satisfying and what driving is all about.

TRAFFIC INCIDENTS

When involved in a road accident, it is vital you follow standard procedure:

- Listen in slow motion to the hideous noise of crunching metal and glass.

- Think to yourself 'That didn't sound very promising'.

- Realise you've just knackered your car, someone else's car, and cost yourself hundreds of pounds.

- Swear.

- Catch your breath, calm down.

- Swear again.

- Panic as you try to remember sending off the insurance renewal.

- Swear again.

- Swear some more.

- Have a really big swear.

- Get out of the car and try to look cool and nonchalant.

- Fail to look cool and nonchalant.

- Try to be nice to the other driver (even though he's a chuffing idiot and clearly at fault for putting his car in the way of yours).

- Examine the damage and realise (1) you're strangely thrilled, (2) you're totally screwed.

- Exchange contact details with the other driver, fighting the urge to give your name as 'Manky Ploppypants'.

- Start rehearsing the dramatic story you're going to give your family and friends.

- Start rehearsing the mundane story you're going to give your insurance company.

- Swear one last time.

- Cry.

Try to be subtle when giving false names.

PETROL STATIONS

When pulling into a petrol station you have 3.3 seconds to decide which queue to join. This requires making an instant character profile of each pump user (taking into account their age, sex, class, and occupation) as well as estimating:

- How much petrol they'll need.

- The size of their petrol tank.

- The ease of replacing the petrol cap.

- The chances of them wasting time wandering around the shop.

- The likelihood of them paying by cash, card, or, heavens forbid, cheque.

DID YOU KNOW...?

Although the French word for 'stop' is '*arrêt*', road signs in France bear the English version of the word. As a result, no one in France has ever stopped.

Drivers should avoid the schoolboy error of getting over-excited and jumping into a surprisingly empty queue. Chances are the pump is out of order and has a weird plastic clamp thing over the handle, forcing you to suffer the ignominy of reversing backwards and joining a new queue while your fellow motorists peer out their windows and gloat.

When fuelling your vehicle, always ensure you have a good look around. Size up the other customers, the people waiting to go next and the misguided bloke queuing for the car wash, and work out whether you are the coolest person there. You probably are – unless you're Richard Hammond.

On no account should you read the adverts on the pump handle. These are incredibly dull and usually about insurance, loyalty schemes, or why their fuel is good for the environment, even though it isn't.

ADDITIONAL RULES
AND GUIDANCE

Always try to fill your petrol tank to a round figure. Whether it's £50 or 50 litres, getting to an exact figure with a series of noughts is immensely satisfying albeit incredibly sad. True experts can hit the magic figure without even resorting to the final trigger bursts of stop/start as you negotiate the last few pence.

It is a legal requirement for petrol stations to have the following:

- A bucket of dying flowers.

- A scary customer in a BMW.

- An outdoor newspaper stand with a large slab of clear plastic for a cover.

- A dopey sales assistant wearing a baseball cap that's slightly too large.

- A female sales assistant who constantly talks to colleagues while serving you.

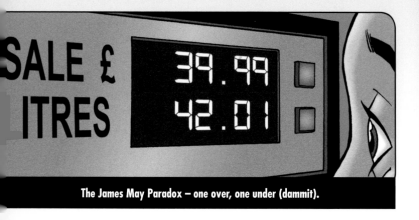

The James May Paradox – one over, one under (dammit).

- The uncanny ability to make you buy mints.

- An air and water machine that sits unloved and idle until the moment that you need it – at which point it's miraculously popular.

- A shortage of milk.

All garage sales assistants must ask whether you'd like a VAT receipt. Even though it's patently obvious you don't because you've just bought £5 worth of petrol, a can of coke and an anaemic ham sandwich that contains less meat than a Linda McCartney sausage.

When leaving the petrol station at motorway services, it is compulsory for the distance between the exit and the feeder lane to be no more than 200 metres, requiring drivers to accelerate from 0–70mph while negotiating HGVs and confused people in Rovers.

DID YOU KNOW...?

82 percent of British drivers involved in a minor accident admitted attempting to avoid an insurance claim by giving the false name 'Dame Judi Dench'.

ADDITIONAL RULES
AND GUIDANCE

MOTOR VEHICLE DOCUMENTATION

DRIVING LICENCE

You **MUST** be in possession of a driving licence. Of course, most teenagers apply for a driving licence the moment they turn 17 for the sole motive of getting into clubs and being served alcohol. Especially useful when the age-old tactic of memorising a false date of birth is undermined by the fact your mathematical incompetence means you're actually passing yourself off as a pensioner.

MOT

Cars and motorcycles **MUST** normally pass a MOT test three years from the date of the first registration and every year thereafter. This tends to involve an agonising wait while a mechanic checks over your beloved heap of crap before delivering an estimate that's twice as bad as you expected and four times as expensive.

How to fix your car while simultaneously destroying your wallet

Did you know that MOT stands for Ministry Of Transport? No, not many people do. That's because it's not especially interesting.

INSURANCE
You **MUST** have a valid insurance policy. In all likelihood you will have got this from a price comparison site (one with an annoying advert that annoying people insist is hilarious). You will have been a little economical with the truth while providing your details, and you will have opted for a damage excess that's way, way higher than you'd like. Finally, you will be consumed with impotent fury when your premium is doubled thanks to the speed fine you picked up for driving through idle road works at midnight on a deserted motorway.

REGISTRATION CERTIFICATE
Registration certificates are issued for all motor vehicles. You **MUST** notify the DVLA when buying or selling a motor vehicle. This is ostensibly to protect you from fraud. Although selling these details on to private clamping firms is a nice little earner for all concerned. Except you, obviously.

DID YOU KNOW...?

The M1 and the M6 were once engaged to be married.

VEHICLE EXCISE DUTY

All motor vehicles used or kept on public roads **MUST** display a valid Vehicle Excise Duty disc. Basically, this is a fancy way of saying you've got to have a tax disc on your windscreen. One of the simple joys of car ownership is watching the coloured ink fade over the course of a year before being replaced by a brand spanking new one. An expensive pleasure, admittedly, but when it comes to chronic exploitation of the motorist, you have to find happiness where you can.

When taxing your vehicle, you will need your registration certificate, a valid MOT certificate, and an original copy of your insurance policy. Finding all three simultaneously is about as easy as a chronic dyslexic passing a spelling test in clinical anatomy (in Hungarian).

Use reputable car dealers

VEHICLE MAINTENANCE AND SAFETY

You **MUST** ensure that your vehicle is roadworthy. Or thereabouts.

You **MUST** keep your windscreen clear and your vehicle clean. Unless you drive a white transit van, in which case leave your vehicle to collect dirt except for the obligatory finger-scribbled slogans 'Clean me,' 'MUFC' and 'Gary is a cock'.

You **MUST** have your vehicle regularly serviced and submitted for its MOT.

When visiting a garage, do your best to look streetwise, knowledgeable and, above all, poor. Use phrases like 'It's a good little runner' even though people in the car trade haven't used that expression since the days of *Minder*.

Avoid phrases like 'I don't know anything about cars…' 'There's a strange sound coming from the front bit…' 'I'll pay whatever it takes…' and 'I'm from the Highways Agency'.

DID YOU KNOW…?

At Christmas, traffic lights are replaced by fairy lights.

PENALTIES

Penalty fines are levied to deter drivers from speeding, illegal parking and other minor offences and most definitely **NEVER, EVER, EVER** to raise cash, hit performance levels, justify expenditure, or compensate for the police officer's low self-esteem.

The perception that motorists and motorcyclists are easy targets for taxation and revenue has been reinforced by several pieces of legislation, including:

- Motor Vehicles (Bullying And Exploitation) Act 2002.

- Earn £££s with a Speed Camera Act 2003.

- Ha Ha Ha, Let's Get The Car-Driving Imbeciles Act 2004.

- Long-Suffering Commuters (Shooting Fish in a Barrel) Regulations 2005.

- £60 Fine For Being Two Minutes Late Leaving a Car Park Order 2006.

- This is Incredible – How Do We Keep Getting Away With This? (Squeezing Blood Out of a Stone While Simultaneously Taking the Piss) Act 2007.

- Massive Parking Fines For Stopping Outside A Station (Even Though They Were Just Dropping Someone Off) Act 2008.

- Pretending Car Taxation is an Incentive to Be More Eco-Conscious (And Absolutely Nothing to Do with Screwing Ordinary Law-abiding Citizens Who Don't Have a Choice) Regulations 2009.

DID YOU KNOW...?

To ease congestion, from 2015 the M6 will become a one-way street.

It is possible to overturn a speeding conviction. However, you will require strong evidence, questionable circumstances, and a bloody good lawyer.

It is not uncommon for celebrities to overturn a speeding offence due to a technicality or loophole exploited by aforementioned lawyer. The public reaction is usually (1) Good on them, or (2) F****** lawyers!

DID YOU KNOW...?

By law, local authorities must help blind drivers by supplying a Braille version of every road sign.

British pubs are full of tattoo-encrusted blokes who reckon you can escape a speeding fine by pretending you can't remember who was driving. These muppets are responsible for millions of people getting speeding fines.

Anyone accumulating more than 12 or more points within a three-year period will be automatically disqualified. That said, newspapers are full of stories about convicted criminals who drive unchallenged for years, despite being disqualified, having no tax, no insurance, and usually no driver's licence. How the police fail to spot these chancers beggars belief. The cars have got a licence plate; the police have got computers. How hard can it be?

In exceptional circumstances a motor vehicle can be confiscated. This can be the result of the offender being imprisoned, deported, or because they own a horrifically crap car. Occasionally it can be due to the offender having a really good car and the police officer being jealous.

If you encounter a car driving at exactly 70mph on a motorway, chances are the motorist is either messing about with their cruise control, a native of Germany, or carrying nine penalty points and terrified of getting three more.

DID YOU KNOW...?

Between 1976 and 1983 Hilton Park services on the M6 received almost no visitors after it was accidentally marked on road maps as 'Unexploded bomb'.

ADDITIONAL RULES
AND GUIDANCE

SIGNS

SIGNALS TO OTHER ROAD USERS

ARM SIGNALS

Cheers mate.

Nice driving.

And I like your
Audi too.

Let's have a full
and frank discussion
about your driving.

I am moron.

I am a very busy
moron.

Tea, anyone?

You will never
guess what my wife
is doing to me
RIGHT NOW.

I'm looking for a CD.

I think I braked too
quickly.

Sorry, officer.

And see you at the
Lodge tonight.

SIGNALS BY AUTHORISED PERSONS

POLICE OFFICERS

Hello, how are you?

It's 3 o'clock.

Since the accident, that's the most I've been able to bend it.

PEOPLE CONTROLLING TRAFFIC

Sorry, I've not perfected this hand swearing thing yet.

Ahhh, the arrow's biting me.

Have you met my invisible wife?

SCHOOL CROSSING PATROLS

Nope, this isn't right.

The tight rope walker.

The return serve.

Ta-dah!

ROAD SIGNS

Urban speed limit.

Rural speed limit.

Strangely pedantic speed limit.

Speed limit for Premiership foot- ballists who are being 'chased by the paparazzi'.

National speed limit.

Phillips' national speed limit.

Sorry, can't re- member this one.

Accelerate.

Sorry, the line- drawing artist is on holiday.

Look, it's Stig in a red helmet!

Optician ahead.

Pie?

SIGNS

Line-drawing car
ahead.

Line-drawing bus
ahead.

Line-drawing artist
ahead.

Out-of-control
two-dimensional
cars ahead.

No, Jeremy, no.

ARGH! Massive
punctuation.

George Michael
attempting to drive
ahead.

Was that your
tortoise?

10% chance of
cheese.

Erm, wasn't this an
Oasis album?

TRAFFIC LIGHTS

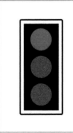	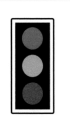	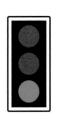	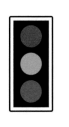
RED – Yawn.	RED & AMBER – 5000rpm.	GREEN – GO, GO, GO!	YELLOW, PURPLE – Traffic lights are playing up.

DIRECTION SIGNS
(IF YOU ARE JAMES MAY)

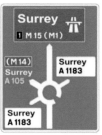

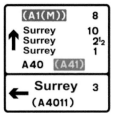

INDEX

TOP GEAR THE ALTERNATIVE HIGHWAY CODE

FURTHER EDITIONS

Top Gear The Alternative Highway Code is now available
in a range of different editions.

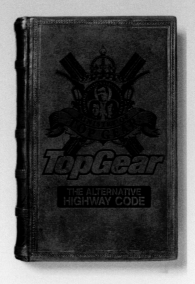

DELUXE EDITION
£199.99

Glossy pages bound in leather from one of
Richard Hammond's tatty jackets. Comes with slip
case, book mark, CD, DVD, and instantly redundant
cassette. Plus a limited edition commemorative road
sign, autographed by the presenters, and bent in
half by the Stig.

EXPANDED EDITION
£99.99
Contains bonus rules, interactive advice,
previously unreleased regulations, and a special
pull-out stretch of tarmac.

BUFF EDITION
£75
Identical to the standard edition but the people in the drawings are stark bollock naked.

MUSICAL EDITION
£50
All rules set to music by Andrew Lloyd Webber and performed by Graham Norton as part of a shameless BBC cash-in.

UPSIDE-DOWN EDITION
£25
Identical to the standard edition but turned upside down.

ECONOMY EDITION
£1.99
No-frills budget version
designed to embarrass
impoverished readers.

RUBBISH EDITION
35P
Bent spine, torn cover,
badly dog-eared, covered
in felt-tip pen and crayon,
with several pages ripped
out. Specially designed for
libraries and charity shops.

BLANK EDITION
£14.99
128 blank pages
for no reason
whatsoever.
Basically, it's a
writing pad at a
vastly overinflated
price.

If you enjoyed this Highway Code, you might enjoy some of our other products and services.

TOP GEAR GUIDE TO BMW TAILGATING

How to get right up someone's backside, especially when you're in slow-moving traffic on the outside lane of the motorway. Includes details of when to flash your headlights, how to dive inside someone at the last possible moment, and how to slam on the brakes and utterly terrify the vehicle behind you.

MAINTAINING YOUR SPACE SHUTTLE

A complete reference manual for owners of home-made space craft. Launch procedures, flight procedures, and crash procedures. Plus how to put pie into a squeezable tube and what to do in the highly unlikely event of finding yourself in orbit.

AIRSHIP CARAVANNING FOR BEGINNERS

Includes tips for treetop avoidance, emergency landings, and how to maintain good relations with passing police helicopters and air traffic control.

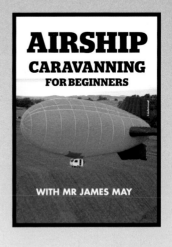

TOP GEAR YSSANAGOG FFARDWR SOGOL I MAWR

Welsh version of the Highway Code. Probably. It's hard to tell whether it's Welsh or just someone choking on a peanut. Contains special advice for Welsh drivers, including tips for parking a horse and carriage, adapting your vehicle to run on coal, and finding the quickest route out of Wales.

KNOW YOUR ROAD MARKINGS

A comprehensive 800-page guide to kerb, carriageway and road markings, and their role in history. At least we think so – no one's ever bothered to read to the end. You lose the will to live around 'Chapter 6: The Evolution of the Double-Spaced Chevron'.

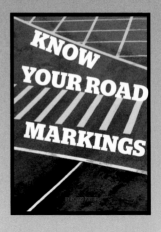

BIRMINGHAM – A CULTURAL HISTORY

Single-page leaflet. Contains large photographs, small photographs, several space-fillers, and directions to Coventry.

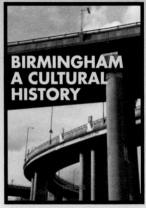

PRACTICAL ADVICE FOR LORRY DRIVERS

Detailed advice on diet (bacon sandwiches), hygiene (wiping your mouth with your sleeve), whistling, driving with one hand while urinating into a bottle, leaning an arm on the window, looking down contemptuously at passing motorists, picking up hitch-hikers, plus remote places to bury them.

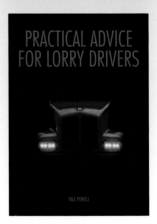